CW01432399

DATE SHOW

First published in 2025 by Blue Diode Press
30 Lochend Road
Leith
Edinburgh EH6 8BS
www.bluediode.co.uk

All rights reserved. No part of this book may be reproduced, stored in a retrieval system, or transmitted in any form, or by any means, electronic, mechanical, photocopying, recording or otherwise, without prior written permission from Blue Diode Press

© Jane Bonnyman

The right of Jane Bonnyman to be identified as author of this work has been asserted in accordance with Section 77 of the Copyright, Designs and Patents Act 1988

ISBN: 978-1-915108-36-4

Typesetting: Rob A. Mackenzie
text in Dante MT Pro

Cover art: 'Jaydid Bird' by Sarah Grant
Design and typography: Rob A. Mackenzie

Diode logo design: Sam and Ian Alexander

Printed and bound by Imprint Digital, Exeter, UK
https://digital.imprint.co.uk

'I want the fairy tale … dammit'
—**Kathryn Bevis**

DATE SHOW

Jane Bonnyman

BLUE DIODE PRESS
Edinburgh

CONTENTS

I

11   Spider-Man: The Final Chapter

12   Storm-Lover

13   La P'tite Folie

14   Drone

15   Lighting Guy

16   Director

17   On Joining the Unmoving Zig Zag Easyjet Queue for the Delayed 12.35 Flight to Bristol and Realising I'm Standing Directly Opposite My Ex and His New Girlfriend

18   Dinner with Superman

19   Dating Dr Jones

20   Cycle-Path

21   Just a Dude

22   Message from a Dog-Lover

23   On Arriving Two Days Later at Bristol Airport to Find My Ex and His New Girlfriend Already Waiting at Gate 16 for the 12.05 Return Flight to Glasgow

24   Weather Man

25   Joe Cool

26   Rogue

27   Solo

28   This Dating Malarkey

29   Material Girl

30   Mug

31   Writer

32   The Look of Love

33   Dream Sequence

34   After Breaking Up With My Neighbour,

35   This Again

II

39 Letter from an Ex (Poetry-Lover)

40 Confidence Man

41 Why he loves Tolkien

42 A Date with Farmer Oak

43 The Whistling Boy

44 Novel Heroines

46 Yet Another Unfortunate Choice

47 Undateable

48 Dear Adam

49 Gatsby

50 Lost World

51 In Your Favourite Café

52 Stuntman

53 Road Trip

55 Baby

56 Untitled (Spinster Caledonia)

57 Bachelor School

58 I'm Trying to Make You Leave Her

59 The Last Word

60 Maybe

61 Date Show

62 Sea-Fishing

65 January

I

Spider-Man: The Final Chapter

When I think of the times you were late, hurling your bike against a railing,
swinging into the café two minutes before closing, still hoping for dinner,
and how one slow morning, you told me your job would always come first,
such is the matter of saving lives – long days and consecutive nights;

it takes me back to our second date when you shrugged off your jumper
to reveal your favourite t-shirt with the giant tarantula drawn on the front.
I screamed because it was bigger than your head, and in the evening light
its legs seemed to move across your chest. 'Got it in Australia,' you said.

And even then, I could picture the comic scene: you in the webbed-mask
and Spandex suit, whisking me between two buildings and up to the stars –
everything hinging on the hero with the fashion sense and superpowers –
and the final shot: the two of us, above the neon city, hanging by a thread.

Storm-Lover

Looking back, I think that year with you
was like being in the final scene from *Twister,*
where I only have time to strap myself to
a water pipe, before I'm whisked into
an F5 tornado, clinging on for dear life
in the chaos of your lost keys, mood
swings and father issues – your words flying
at my face and stinging like shrapnel,
until you chuck me out and zoom off
towards Double Creek, and I'm left in
some field, watching the sky clear, and it's quiet
enough to hear the cowbirds calling from
the undergrowth and my friends
pulling up in their cars,
telling me to be more
careful, and in future
I should head for
the storm cellar,
as soon as
the weather-
vane spins
and the land-
breeze
ruffles
the
cor
n

.

La P'tite Folie

When, on our blind date in the French restaurant,
while you're telling me about your six-day hike
through the wilderness of the Southern Alps,
I lean towards you and set fire to my hair,
accidently dipping it into the candle flame,

you watch as if it were happening on a screen:
me clutching a damp napkin to my head,
sweeping the singed strands from the tablecloth,
apologising for the mess. Somewhere Piaf sings
'Non, je ne regrette rien,' and you ask for the bill.

And I think I always knew, the way some things
seem to be meant, that it would end like this:
one half-eaten soufflé, me working out the tip,
and the chill from the open door as you,
already in your coat, run for the hills.

Drone

I've just bought a new toy, he tells me,
a multicopter, the camera attached by
a gimbal stabiliser, which tilts mid-flight,
making it super easy to get the classic
bird's eye view of the town at golden hour,
and another documenting coastal erosion.
Of course, he goes on, there's so much more –
the 36 page e-book explains how to adjust it
to a higher frame to record in slow motion,
and, depending on the setting, it'll hover,
fly backwards or orbit around a central
location, like the beginning of *Shawshank*
when you look down on the grey prison
and see inmates streaming across the yard,
or the scenes of Manhattan in *Spiderman*.
I'm not saying I could do that, he admits,
but it's important to have goals and a plan.
The main thing is to write a list of shots
before filming, because if you're not careful,
you'll waste the battery on long and tedious
footage that gets in the way of the story.

Lighting Guy

We meet on Zoom, one evening, in April.
He goes through his career, how he studied
Lighting Design at RADA and did a stint
at the Old Vic Theatre, before moving on
to The Royal Ballet. He's won Baftas for
his work on Beckett's *Waiting for Godot*
and for strobe effects in a minimalist
staging of *The Crucible*. I say that's fantastic,
incredible, he must be extremely talented,
but now I'm staring at the screen, trying
to make him out from the shadows of
his living room, because wherever he is
in Kent, dusk is falling, and I tell him
it's as if he's sitting inside a wardrobe,
or at the bottom of a disused mineshaft.
Yeah, sorry, he laughs, his desk lamp
has broken and the over-head bulb went
last month, so he's there in the dark.
Anyway, he wants to talk about me and
English teaching? Do I find it rewarding,
or is it just all spelling and apostrophes,
and finding good examples of irony.

Director

When we hug goodbye, he says
'Lips' and we kiss. It's perfunctory,
like reaching up to dust the light
or water the plant on the dresser.

I'd met him before, once, to discuss
education, resourcing, council funding,
but now we're standing on the platform,
while folk wheel past cases and lug children.

He has to go. Glasgow by 4pm. Emails to send.
He leans in again. I break away, telling him
I have to get shoes. We speak about shoes.
He stares at his brogues. Top quality.
So bloody comfy. Got them in Italy.

For God's sake just get on the train.

On Joining the Unmoving Zig Zag Easyjet Queue for the Delayed 12.35 Flight to Bristol and Realising I'm Standing Directly Opposite My Ex and His New Girlfriend

Fuck.

Dinner with Superman

For a good hour I've been studying him –
the suede brogues, designer jeans
the crisp white shirt and the gleaming teeth
of that all-American smile. I think I love him:
the foal-brown of his eyes; the touch of his skin
as he picks up the bill. 'I'll get this,' he insists.
His voice is like a breeze, drifting through
timothy in a far-off prairie. He asks to walk me
home, and once outside, I notice his height –
so tall his head brushes the lining of clouds.
And when we reach my tenement, he looks
around for his date. 'Goodbye,' he says,
glancing down, 'I've got an early morning flight.'
I stand in front of my door like a Lego woman,
my arm raised in the posture of a wave.
In the distance the red flash of a cape.

Dating Dr Jones

Although I don't care for Aztec tombs,
or dining on baby snakes and monkey-
brains and finding eyeballs in my soup,
I can't help joining the crusade, to see him
solve mysteries and win against the Nazis –
Dear God the way his strong arms haul him
from the deepest ravine, and how he dodges
that mammoth boulder chasing him through
the tunnel and emerges still wearing his fedora.

This is a man with his own theme-tune,
who'll bring a bowl of apples to your room,
and quite soon, you know he'll move on,
that there's a new woman in every film,
and yet it's worth it for a fling, a thrilling affair,
like stealing a sacred stone or the Holy Grail,
but then he slips up and sets off a trap,
and you have to split before the walls start
closing in and the temple crashes down.

Cycle-Path

Dusk, mid-November, and I'm wandering
through the park, studying the sunset,
and thinking about my mother,
when, out of nowhere, he whizzes past
on his Rockrider 900 and yells 'Cycle-path!',
giving me the fright of my life,
because I've strayed over the line,
and now he must alert me to his presence,
as if I hadn't already noticed
the windproof vest, padded tights,
head torch and tail-lights flashing,
like a low-flying military jet,
and how he's only got a few miles to go
before he beats his personal best,

and later he'll add his time to a spreadsheet,
or PowerPoint, that he'll try to show
some girl on a date. He'll tell her
life is like the Tour de France: a series
of hair-pin bends and endurance tests,
and, afterwards, outside the pub, she'll wait
while he unclips the anti-theft lock
from the front wheel and puts on
his aerodynamic helmet and Thermo gloves.
He'll say he'd offer to walk her home,
if it wasn't for his bike and the fact that
he can get back in less than ten minutes
if he takes the route by the defunct railway track –
the one he looked up earlier on his navigation app.

Just a Dude

looking for laughs & a partner
in crime – no bunny boilers
or drama please, or anyone with
an A-level in arguing & hysteria,
& no cats, kids or feminists.
I'm stress-free & need similar,

the kind of woman who'll fix
my bike rack & massage
my shoulders, who'll bring me
a cold beer, after a hard day
engineering global finance,
or swimming the channel.

She must love dogs & tacos.
I don't have time for pen pals
or bullshit. My mates say I can
be a knobhead, a bit of a pirate,
but at least I'm funny lol 😊
& don't take life too serious.

I'm into campervans & travel.
And though I've got a few miles
on the clock & have to pluck
the odd hair from my ear lobes,
I'm still a lad at heart – I want
to be an astronaut when I grow up.

Message from a Dog-Lover

Each afternoon during autumn
we go for a walk, Millie and me,
in the South Pennines or the Dales –
we love to get out of the city.
She's being a right monkey tonight
jumping on the computer as I type this –
would you like to take her off my hands?
(Just kidding). Yesterday, she ate cow pellets
in the field and now she's feeling ropey.
Poor girl! Yeah, would be good to chat,
our messages are getting longer and longer,
the weekend sounds grand, here's my number –

but, I should probably say that when you call
I'm likely to chicken out and not answer.
Then it'll be time for Millie's jaunt in the garden,
and I don't like being on the phone after nine,
so perhaps it's better if you didn't bother.
You see the dog is non-negotiable,
and she likes her routine. If you stayed over,
she'd sprawl across her side of the bed,
so you'd have to sleep in the other room.
Oh, and she doesn't like drama,
or neediness and folk who lie in.
Both of us get up at dawn.

On Arriving Two Days Later at Bristol Airport to Find My
Ex and His New Girlfriend Already Waiting at Gate 16 for
the 12.05 Return Flight to Glasgow

Double Fuck.

Weather Man

Not those months spent
in Texas and New Orleans,
studying the impact of a hurricane,
or the time you scaled the inside
of a wind turbine to fix a cable
and measure the blade rotation,
or the tornado you chased
in an act of derring-do
across the Great Plains;

rather it was the night
when you stopped by a shop window,
on the way to the restaurant,
to check out your hair, your scarf,
the lie of your coat and muttered
'Lookin' good'... under your breath –
that image of you, there, beside me
winking and hi-fiving the glass
was what really blew me away.

Joe Cool

When he talks about buying new clothes,
he means in the summer of the next millennia,
at the end of the closing down sale, just before
they whitewash the windows, board up the door,

or he'll wait for his mother to give him
a pair of trousers that don't sag to his ankles,
or for his boss to notice the flecks of toothpaste
spattered like paint on his waterproof,

and even then, he'll only think about it,
the way he thinks about hoovering
and binning the dead Christmas tree,
or clearing the dishes from the sink,

and he wants me to go with him,
because I know all the shops and how
to stop him from choosing the jumper
the colour of Irn Bru, or the Snoopy t-shirt

that says 'Nope. Not today' on the front,
with the picture of the dog taking it easy
in the sun, while the yellow bird sits beside him
chirping, and flapping its tiny wings.

Rogue

And though you planned all of it meticulously,
booking the bar and tapas place, getting a 2 for 1
deal on the film tickets, keeping time so we left
the restaurant at 7.26pm to walk to the cinema,

you couldn't have foreseen the twist in events:
the lad lurching from the towpath in the dark,
evidently off his face, the one who followed us
and lunged for your wallet outside the IMAX,

but who, thankfully, missed, and then slumped
to the floor inside the revolving door, and got
stuck between the moving glass, yelling FFS!
as it whacked him intermittently on the arse.

You won't have known it would end with you
sipping lemonade in the foyer, and me saying
not to worry, at least you're ok, and whatever
happens, this will always make a good story.

Solo

When, in the middle of the restaurant,
and quite without warning, he whips out his
ukelele and plays 'Sur le Pont d'Avignon',
I begin to reconsider the evening,

and later, in the club, while he shimmies
across the dancefloor, plucking the strings
in syncopation to 'Pump up the Jam',
I get the feeling he's not the one,

and, finally outside the chip shop,
as he serenades the parked cars, the bus stop,
a passing fox, I say I'd rather just be friends.
But's he's not listening,

he's working through his favourite songs.
'Music is the love of my life!' he shouts,
and I tell him I'm heading home.
'No! Don't go!' he pleads, taking my hand.

He wants us to team up, do an album –
it'd be such fun. He'll lead the vocals
and hold the tune and I'll be in the background
on a tambourine, or bongo drum.

This Dating Malarkey

Round & round the gooseberry tree
& through the torrible glen
until you find him & oh what fun!
for a time, cavorting like river mice
& building a home, but then he runs
off with a dish & it all falls down,

& though you're over the hill & a glum
sugar-plum, you go off to market to swipe
through ten thousand men – all billy goats
& sniffle bores & everyone laughs to hear
your tales from the sorogroves, thanking
their silly-stars they're not in Singly Wood,

like the Jaydid bird who spends her days
laying out her display of bric-a-brac
& broken things & calloohs & callays
for Faraway-Jack, for Not-A-Prat-Jack
to come swishing in & ask her to dance,
by the light of the calico moon.

Material Girl

When, at last, I meet a man
who has a stunning three-bed flat,
equipped with heated floors
and a claw-foot bath,
he turns out to be a psychopath.

Mug

The day after I told him I'd treasure it,
raving about it being the perfect present,
I lost my grip and smashed it on the radiator,
the blue handle going to pieces
and scuttling across the floor.

Strange that it takes a moment like this
to make you re-consider the facts:
how he dug it out of some badly-packed box,
before his five-month trip to New York,
and wrapped it as a token to compensate

for all the let downs, the talk of his ex;
and that only, as a last resort,
when he'd finished his important tasks,
two G&Ts and a gallon of Chablis,
did he ever come near me;

and now, I wonder why I'm hanging on
like some die-hard fan, waiting for him
to appear in his well-chosen suit
for another performance –
'Encore! Encore!' I yell from the back,

as he moves through the audience,
shaking hands, hugging friends,
and I'm there in my green dress
and kitten heels, clapping and waving.
Look at me waving.

Writer

After he told me
that once in a pavement café
in the Place de la Bastille
when, in conversation with friends,
he threw his head back to laugh,
and a pigeon shat in his mouth,
I could not kiss him.

He wrote poetry with French words,
said my eyes glinted like malachite.

It didn't work.
I just thought he was full of it.

The Look of Love

'Would you like Dusty or Nat King Cole?' you ask,
and I realise the line's rehearsed –
you've spent the afternoon laying out, in order,
the hits you hoped I'd like,
and suddenly the bowl of potato salad,
the red wine on the shelf,
the two cat mugs next to the kettle give you away,
and I'm sitting in a room where flowers,
scatter cushions, the positioning of chairs
are waiting for an unwritten scene,
and if I turned on my heels they would grow tiny legs,
like the dish and the spoon, and chase me
into the night calling 'Don't go! Don't ever go!'

Dream Sequence

Which brings me back to your tenement.
Stone steps. Stained glass. Wild geraniums.
A green bike tied to the banister.
A canoe propped against the wall.
Tall windows thrown open
to the December night.

You're on the fifth floor,
pulling her close, whispering into her ear.
A photo frame faces down on the piano.
I give up on the stairs and summon a ladder,
like the one that might descend from a UFO.
A close-up of my fingers, grasping the metal rung.

Now you're in the bedroom, pulling clothes
from drawers, piling jumpers into a case.
I want to go to you,
but there's a black storm door.
My eye moves to the keyhole,
and the whole flat's on fire.

White flames swallow the hat-stand.
A helicopter lands in the hall.
And before you take off through the roof,
you ask me what I'm doing there.
My casual answers. 'Just passing.'
'Came to return the key.' 'Saw your light was on.'

After Breaking Up With My Neighbour,

I summon the Statue of Liberty
from *Ghostbusters II* and bring her
to life with kinaesthetic slime
and that classic R&B song,
blaring round her steel frame.

Then, from inside the crown,
I watch as she strides along my street,
and when we pass his house, I look
down and wave, while she flattens
his car with her huge sandaled feet.

And once back at mine, I abseil onto
the lawn and turn to thank her for
getting me home, but she's already off,
carrying her torch above the rooftops,
the blue flowers of the empress tree.

This Again

Now that the roof sags like plasticine, rooms are full of gloop
and the walls bulge and slump, and everyone agrees it's no use,
we ditch the thing and split. You brush it off like you always do
and zoom between trees, across the river and vanish into moorland
to seek out another mate in the heather, while I hover, trying to heal,
then, finally, zip over hills and hedgerows, before hunkering down
in the woodpile. After years of fails and fiascos, I'm quick to pad
the sides with grubs and leaflitter and burrow deep into the tunnel,
because I know all about winter and this being alone, again etc.

II

Letter from an Ex (Poetry-Lover)

Hey! Great to hear from you.
Yes, I'm still into poetry, but
since I last saw you, I've not read
much, apart from a few titles in
Waterstones, and though I must say
the books I chose were excellent,
I've lost the hunger, the urge to
write, because, you see, I've fallen
in love, and it's stopped me in
my tracks. We've been together
for two years, and now we share
a flat, and, tbh, I'm just so happy,
and also, I've been promoted to
Assistant Head at work, which is
a brilliant job, and I'm crazily busy!

And what about you? I take it you've
carried on writing. I remember
you in that garden shed, sitting
at the desk you'd pulled from a skip
staring out at the plum tree,
the sparrows in the hedge, waiting
on inspiration. Please let me know
when you've finished a collection,
and maybe we could meet up
if I happen to be in Edinburgh?
I mean, Laura (that's my girlfriend)
often performs in the festival –
in some ways, you're quite similar,
except she likes politics and history
and she has no time for poetry.

Confidence Man

wears a coat by Dolce Gabbana
and sits astride a Triumph motorbike,
ready to tear into the Arrochar Alps
for some pine-scented air and time

away from his schedule, jam-packed
with living the dream: the movies,
charity work, million-dollar book deals,
the homes in LA, New York, Melbourne.

In a suede jacket and trainers by Boss
he talks about his early acting career:
those iconic moments for his character.
He opens the top button of his shirt

and poses for the camera, then leaps
from a warehouse roof in Shoreditch,
lands in the centre of the street, stopping
the traffic with his cherry leather boots.

He admits he's just happy in his own skin
and speaks about the moon's effect on how
things manifest. 'We're made of stardust,'
he says, smiling, as if we all had it in us.

Why he loves Tolkien

First, the wide-angle shots of snow-covered peaks
with scope for high-altitude climbing and extreme
camping on the Southern slopes. Then, of course,
the quest, old as Odysseus, the never-settling: canoe-
trips on the River Anduin, nights spent in Gondor,
Rohan and the Withered Heath, swapping stories
round the fire of legends and daring exploits. Plus,
there's the thrill of wielding an axe or broad sword,
the chance to dispatch a few orcs with a crossbow,
and stamp an illuminated staff into the ground
in an act of machismo that will see off any dragon,

but, really, it's because this is a tale about a ring
and a band of men with such fear of commitment
they're willing to face a giant spider, nine Black Riders
and ghosts of dead kings, to journey through Mordor,
right into the blazing depths of Mount Doom, just so
they can finally be rid of the thing; because deep down
they don't want a relationship and would rather go back
to their one-bed flat and live out of a rucksack, dining
on ready meals and craft beer, until some mate drops by
with plans for a new adventure: bungee-jumping into
the abyss, or an eternal hike up the Lonely Mountain.

A Date with Farmer Oak

He can predict the weather by a slight shift in cloud,
a toad slumped in the doorway, a rook's uneasy call.

He traces his thumb along the jawbone of a skull,
half-buried in heather, and pronounces it 'hare',

then points out a lapwing, a buzzard feather,
star flowers, bog myrtle, unusual rock formations.

He walks for hours without water, slings his tired dog
onto his shoulder as if it were a new born lamb.

Later, during dinner, I ask about life in Dorset,
his father, his love of folk music; but he won't answer.

Instead, he slices a clean line through his burger,
and pierces each chip exactly in the centre.

Once finished, he looks up and tells me
he's sorry but he doesn't eat and talk.

'It's ok,' I reply, 'there's a silence that says much.'
Outside, the sky grows darker than oil cloth.

He leaves without pudding.
He must see to the barley and wheatstacks.

From the window, I watch him stride away
in his waxed jacket, collar up against the wind.

The Whistling Boy

a cento from Lorna Moon's Dark Star

They said he owned fourteen shirts, twelve pairs of socks,
and that he could whistle ten operas from start to finish.
One day I'll be a great composer, he told her.
I'll play things like water and the sky.
And she listened, mesmerised.

But he left for Germany and France,
and she stayed at home and wept.
Of course, she hated him: he was the kind of boy
who had his name embroidered in gold on his underpants
and yet... and yet ...

Novel Heroines

four centos from Jane Austen

I

Elizabeth was a good deal disappointed:
he talked only of his friends, his sister
and his flaming horse.
She could think of nothing but Mr Wickham
and those nights in Edward Street
when he wore his best regimentals,
his eye lashes so remarkably fine.

II

Emma feared
his greatest deficiency was in the pencil.
He said it measured six,
but it could not be more than four.
To ease her spirits, she took comfort
in the proper number of balls,
and resolved never to fret
about such a little thing as this.

III

And though she was struck by his genius
Catherine was not thinking of
falling in love,
she preferred cricket, baseball
and rolling down the green slope
at the back of the house

IV

Because she had no desire
to marry her cousin,
as soon as Fanny acquired a horse,
she escaped to the Mediterranean,
where she delighted in the sparkling sea,
aromatic wine and a handsome Count
who possessed good teeth
and twenty thousand pounds.

Yet Another Unfortunate Choice

after Wendy Cope

I would marry Robert Louis Stevenson
and sail with him to wild and distant shores,
if it weren't for that damned American,
and the fact he's been dead since 1894.

Undateable

half a jar
of tomato sugo
in the fridge door
cherry red
after so many months

sits beside
the mustard pot
with a stuck lid
sprouted garlic
a white lemon

Dear Adam

If, on the trip I never made to Oxford, I chance
upon you in the languages section of Blackwell's,
while scanning the spines for your latest book:
Proust: The Life, In Search of Lost Time Explained,
or, one autumn evening, as light slips
from the scene, I run into you in Bloomsbury,
hugging a flute of irises to your coat;

or by some twist of fate, I end up next to you
on the 13.13. to Paris, and you glance at me
in between writing an essay on Villon,
and speaking on the phone to Céline,
who has missed you and is cooking lamb
to go with the bottle of Saint-Julien
you'll pick up on your way home;

if we meet again, I'd like to tell you
that you won't know who I am, except
as a picture that flickers across a screen,
the way I imagine each version of you
wheeling into life like characters on a zoetrope
until it's hard to remember the you I met
so long ago, that July in Edinburgh

when, for a moment, the world tilted
and veered from its usual course.
What was the sound of your voice?
And your eyes – were they garnet brown
or a darker quartz?

P.S. I hope you never read this.

Gatsby

It's the 1920s and you're on the Queen Mary, bound
for New York. I imagine you in the Grand Lobby under
the Art Deco ceiling, summoning a steward to take you to
your cabin: a stateroom with velvet cushions, chaise longue,
champagne and a picture window – half-sky, half-ocean.

Later you order the salmon and potato dauphinoise.
The quartet plays, and you buy a round for the table
and dance with a stranger who wears silk and chiffon.
By day, you go to the cinema and swim in the heated pool.
Sometimes you sit on deck and stare into the grey water,

considering your colossal error – jilting your greatest lover.
After dinner, a bell rings, the captain's voice on the tannoy
says the ship is about to pass over the RMS Titanic,
and you think of the swollen wreck rusting in the depths,
then you down another highball and return to the bar,

where the waiter is reaching up to unhook the clock.
Each night he rewinds it an hour, a novelty at first perhaps,
this repeating the past, but it's become habit, like the way
you slip into thought, swirling the ice around your glass,
insisting what you had was perfect, your life all mapped out,

but now you drink too much, and I know, despite your gifts
and flowers, that you're always waiting, arms outstretched
in the dark, hoping she'll come back, so you can walk together
on blue lawns, thinking it's real: the huge house, the too-pink
bougainvillea, the willow seeds that float in the air like moths.

Lost World

And when I wonder if we should give it
another shot, I think of *Jurassic Park*
and the cost of digging up the past –
how, at first, it seems as if it might work:
the triceratops grazing in the star grass,
the brachiosaurus arching its neck into
the cassia tress and calling like a child;
but soon a storm arrives, and something
feels off, like seeing the mangled fence
of the T-Rex pen, or getting stranded
in a touring truck, watching the water
tremble in those plastic cups, knowing
we'll both have to be helicoptered out,
before it bursts through the gristle ferns
and tears us apart with its tiny hands.

In Your Favourite Café

I snuck in here
when I wasn't looking,
found myself sitting
by the window, staring
at the smudged glass,
the letters spelling
COFFEE back to front.

I see you in an empty chair,
picking at the icing
on your Empire biscuit.
Milky foam clings
to the sides of your cup.
You're wearing your old scarf
and the jumper I bought for you.

It's when I almost hear
the familiar rhythms of your voice,
I realise I'm waiting on the past
to tell me the thing I never quite got,
but I pick up my bag,
and am through the door,
before you know I was there.

Stuntman

Always lost in thoughts of
zipwires and roof-to-roof jumps,
he never looks me in the eye,
preferring the sideways glance
to weigh up danger.

There have been past escapes:
leaping from trains, supermarkets,
backflipping out of restaurants,
and bus shelters, or hiding
under layers of jumpers.

One evening I give him a lift,
and while the car waits at the lights,
I tell him about my life.
We listen to the indicator ticking,
the arrow signalling left, left.

It might need a few takes
to capture the seat belt's arc in mid-air,
the way one hand scoops up
his laptop, bag and coffee cup,
while he kicks open the door.

In a whirlwind I hardly register,
he vanishes into night streets,
and I won't see him again,
unless there's a chance meeting
on a plane, or at a poetry reading.

Road Trip

Seeing you on the dating app
a few months after we broke up
looking like a Greek god,
in a new jacket, power-posing
on a mountaintop, and laughing
with friends I don't know
in a beachside restaurant
that's probably in Saint Lucia,
Santorini or Cape Town,

makes me feel like I've been
sucker-punched in the chest
by an invisible baboon,
or a tectonic plate has shifted
under my chair, and I've fallen
through the floor into the abyss,
and I'm to spend the afternoon,
grasping at tree roots and flint,
trying to haul myself back,

while picturing those scenes
in my mind when you meet her
in some pub, or go for dinner,
and she's as slim as a gazelle
in a strapless dress and heels,
and you take her on a road trip
to the Highlands, like the one
we never went on, through
the pine forests and glens,

and this time she doesn't ask
about your childhood,
or why you don't want to commit,
so you allow her to thread

her arm through yours and walk
along the path that skirts the loch
with the mysterious island in the centre,
so hard to reach, as it is, surrounded
by tall reeds and dangerous waters.

Baby

Because of that summer when he took you from the corner
and taught you the Mambo, the Cha Cha and all about love,

you ditch the Peace Corps and top university course to sit
on the porch, waiting for him to swing by in his Chevrolet,

and drive you into the mountains, just as the sun is slipping
behind the maples and the heron glides across the lake.

Untitled (Spinster Caledonia)

She looks beyond the kailyard and midden,
beyond the aged frame to that day full of sun,
sitting with him on the beach at Stonehaven,
when she felt as if she were outside herself,
watching the beginning of things: the sand
spilling through her fingers; the herring gulls
calling from the cliff; the sea scattering
cowrie shells across the shore; and God!
she never thought years later she'd end up
stuck in a blanket bog, among the sedge
and deergrass, wondering whose fault it was,

and though she knows it's more to do
with untaken paths and the fear she's kept
for so long wrapped in a thornproof cloth,
she finds it easier just to put it down to
the weather, the months of rain and smirr,
or sometimes, like those other wearied Scots,
she blames the English for her hard luck –
the lonely croft and its failing crops –
and for all the fishing trips, back and forth,
in her salt-worn boat, only to bag nothing,
but the odd sprat or common whelk.

Bachelor School

after Kim Hyesoon

I work at a bachelor school.
In this city, it is one of the last schools
that trains bachelors to become eligible.
I lecture in communication and miscellaneous skills.
I run conversation classes in café bars and lead workshops on texting
and synonym writing for bachelors to practise finding other words
for 'babe', 'hot' and 'chillin' with my mates'.
I make them do rounds of 12 bicep curls with laundry bags,
followed by 50 deadlifts with a selection of casserole pans.
I make them unlearn football scores, the names of American Presidents.
I make them uncount the number of mountains they have climbed,
then I teach them how to lie down on the cushion moss
and contemplate the sparrowhawk and field vole,
the pebble loosening itself from the path.
I teach them how to decipher their emotions, studying each one carefully
the way they might slide a rare vinyl from its sleeve and hold it to the light.
I teach them how to open a car bonnet and tell me
they see the heart of a beluga whale.
I have no ulterior motive,
other than to repair the damage done by *The Big Lebowski* –
(a bachelor who lives in shorts/sweatpants may never proceed
beyond foundation level).
At the end of term two, I announce that to qualify for
the Advanced Certificate, a bachelor must complete units on removing
limescale and cleaning Formica, and cook three meals from scratch.
It is usual for most bachelors to drop out; only a select few will graduate –
those who shine like bullet cufflinks and polished brogues.
They'll be snapped up like mangosteen.
Years later, they'll stop me on the street and say
their happiness is stratospheric. They'll write thank you cards and send
them to my office in the old quad where I've been for the past 20 years,
at the top of the gothic tower, up the C18th spiral stair,
and far away from the action.

I'm Trying to Make You Leave Her

I want you to walk out
during dinner,

to hurl her best carbonara
at the wall.

I am hoping you'll turn on
your heels, yelling 'Adios!'

and come back to me,
contrite as a honey bear.

I hope to bow my head
like a Jedi knight

and pop you in the cabinet
beside the glass antelopes.

I want to polish you
on bank holidays

with lemon and vinegar
until you're beautiful –

your face in my hands
smooth as olive shell.

The Last Word

Because I got food poisoning
from your salmon pasta
and burnt my hand spectacularly
on your oven door;

because the first time you stayed over
you whacked your head on
the sloped ceiling in my bedroom
and promptly killed the moment,

and because you went skiing
with your mates and broke your shoulder,
and for weeks you wore a padded sling
the size of a small sofa,

it would be easy to write off
the whole thing as a series of failures,
as if the universe had turned against
us like a disapproving parent,

were it not for that night
in the bar on St Stephen's Street,
when you put down your glass
and said we should kiss

then, later, back at mine
we lit the fire and threw the cushions
on the floor, not caring about the storm
outside the window, or the cyclonic rain.

Maybe

after Paul MacCartney

If you'd taught yourself guitar, aged 14,
trying out chords in the downstairs loo,

if you'd scrawled lyrics onto napkins, plane-tickets,
and could pick up any instrument and lead a band;

if you ditched the bachelor pad, the unfed cats,
dying plants and that mould-rimmed bath,

if you looked at me with laughing eyes
and wrote a song, saying I'm the only woman,

or if you bought a house in the country
with wild orchids and Sussex hens – maybe then.

Date Show

Just as I'm listening to you talking
about your start-up tech company
at the end of another singles' evening,
I suddenly realise I'm on a film set,
and the barman in the Ramones t-shirt,
the DJ and spider plants are all
well-chosen props, and if I shot
an arrow into the top left corner
the whole scene would crumble,
and I'd see a strange light appearing
between the ceiling tiles and hear a voice
calling my name, saying I'm the star
of a TV show that's streaming live on
Channel 4, and everyone's watching,

and I'd run into the street, across
the bridge and out of the city
to escape the sonorous words of
the series creator who's explaining
his plans for future episodes: the one
with the Ferris wheel and mini golf,
or the blind date in the chicken shop,
and he begs me to come back
because of the record viewing figures,
but by now I've reached the edge
where the sagebrush meets the cloud line,
so I bow to the audience and tell them
I want something more, then I push open
the door in the sky and step through.

Sea-Fishing

And if I'm asked about my love life,
I'll say it's like that scene from *Jaws*
when they catch the wrong shark
and show it off like a prize,
thanking God the search is over;
but, of course, Hooper has his doubts,
insisting it doesn't quite measure up,
so that night he and Brody slit it open
and discover fish heads, a tin can,
a Louisiana licence plate,
and the two men sit in a pool of brine
with a torch and the realisation
that it's not easy,
and somewhere, out there,
in the grey ocean, is the one,
and it'll take more than
a day's fishing to catch the rogue,
they'll have to plan a whole expedition
with scuba tanks, barrels and darts –
and they're going to need a bigger boat.

January

Although some days
I can't understand you,
and you don't seem to get me,
we push on regardless
through red alerts and freak storms,
circling the Old Town in gale-force winds,
heading to the Pentlands in Siberian snow,
and you're always there to guide me
across the ice and up the steepest hill
where we balance our makeshift sledge
on the frozen slope and look down,
wondering about rocks and sudden dips,
but you turn to me in your bobble hat
and say we should go for it,
before the light fades
and the rain sweeps in
from the West.

Notes

'Just a Dude' is a cento made up of lines taken from various profiles on a popular dating app.

'This Dating Malarkey' uses 'caloohs' and 'callays' from 'Jabberwocky' by Lewis Carroll.

'A Whistling Boy' uses lines from Lorna Moon's novel *Dark Star*, Bonnier Books, 2002

'Novel Heriones' uses lines from Jane Austen's *Pride and Prejudice, Northanger Abbey, Mansfield Park* and *Emma*.

'I'm Trying to Make You Leave Her,' was inspired by the poem 'I'm Trying to Break Your Heart' by Kevin Young.

'Bachelor School' was inspired by the poem 'Ghost School' by Kim Hyesoon and follows a similar structure.

Acknowledgements

Many thanks to the editors of the following publications in which some of these poems first appeared: *Poetry Scotland, Atrium, Sogo Magazine, The Dark Horse, The Interpreter's House, Magma* and *Poetry Wales*. Several of the poems in this collection were published in my pamphlet *Dinner with Superman* (Red Squirrel Press: 2020).

'This Again' was highly commended in the 'Love and Loss' Competition for *The Passionfruit Review* in March 2025.

Huge thanks to my editor, Rob A. Mackenzie, for believing in and overseeing this collection.

And to Jonathan Edwards, for his ongoing inspiration and his brilliant course on 'Poetry, Art & Pop Culture' run by The Writing School in 2023 and also to Caroline Bird for her fast-paced, zingy triumph of workshop as part of the 'Rise Up! programme in York.

To Mark, Ayshé, Bryana, Sam and everyone at *Pulse Kitchen & Eatery*, Edinburgh, for their tremendous support and the best food in town.

To Sarah Grant (https://www.sarah-grant.com) for her wonderful friendship and for her glorious painting of the 'Jaydid bird' featured on the cover, and to Gail and Richie for their generosity and specialist photographic skills.

Loving thanks to Rhona, Andrea and Anne for their unfailing encouragement, and to Nick for always being there – for all the walks and wisdom.

To my Uncle Gordon for supporting and believing in my creative endeavours.

And to Mum and Dad. Thank you for everything.

Jane Bonnyman is a poet and teacher from Edinburgh. Her work has been widely published in journals including *Mslexia*, *The Frogmore Papers* and *The Rialto*. She has an MA in Creative Writing from Newcastle University, and has published two pamphlets *An Ember from the Fire* (Poetry Salzburg, 2016) and *Dinner with Superman* (Red Squirrel Press, 2020). *Date Show* is her first full collection.